Conquer Your Stress at Work

Table of Contents

Dedication

This book is dedicated to everyone at work. I feel you. I've had jobs where I sat all day, jobs where I stood all day, and jobs where I carried heavy awkward stuff. I've had horrible bosses that drove me to therapy and have run my own business where you lie awake at night wondering if you are going to make rent. I've scrounged for change in my car for gas money and borrowed $5.00 from friends so I could eat dinner. I've faced medical challenges and watched my mother die from cancer while my dad ran his own business and tried to figure out how to manage a teenage me.

I'm Type-A. Okay, I'm Type-A +++++, so I feel you. I know the competitive, driven, controlling, anal-retentive person that is reading this thinking that stress is ok. That stress gives you the edge you need. That you're not working hard enough if you don't feel like you're going out of your mind. And I'm here to tell you, it doesn't have to be that way. I wrote this book with you in mind. Because I want you to be successful, abundant, prosperous…and alive to enjoy it all. To have a long, healthy and full existence. So, for all of you, the head execs and the worker bees, I wrote this book. Enjoy!

And special thanks to my husband Michael for allowing my only-child, Capricorn, Type A, control-freak, driven self to thrive.

Kathy Gruver, PhD
Santa Barbara, CA

Also, a reminder that I am **NOT** a medical doctor and this book is not meant to take the place of your health care provider. I am not intending to diagnose or treat any illness.

Introduction

Thanks so much for reading *Conquer Your Stress at Work.* You are holding this book in your hand; so obviously, you care about your health. Or someone close to you cares about your health. Depending on the age you begin and end employment and what type of job you have, the average person spends 109,980 hours at work in their lifetime. And here's some more info:

- It's estimated that 60-80% of all doctor's visits are from stress-related illness such as depression and heart disease. Those diseases alone cost businesses between $200-$300 billion a year in lost productivity.
- One million workers miss work everyday from stress. This costs over $602/employee per year.
- According to the American Psychological Association, 67% of Americans say work is their top stressor.
- 60% of workers in one survey admitted to losing productivity to stress in the past month.
- Stress lowers our immune system's efficiency, which can increase the susceptibility to colds and flu.
- When people are stressed, they often turn to unhealthy foods and high calorie snacks. In a Career Builder survey, almost 67% of employees admitted to eating unhealthy snacks once a day; 25% said they did at least twice a day.
- A recent Attitudes in the American Workplace poll showed the following: 35% of workers say that their job is harming them physically or emotionally, 36% said they felt they could not express their concerns to their superiors, and 30% felt that management was not sensitive to the needs, conflicts, or problems of stress.
- Large corporations are learning that de-stressed employees are happier and more productive: GlaxoSmithKline, Bank of America, Johnson and Johnson, American Express, Google, Hewlett Packard, PepsiCo and GE are a just a few companies that offer stress and wellness programs.
- When we are stressed, we don't sleep as well or function at our optimum during the day. Sleepiness or lack of concentration leads to industrial and automobile and more slip and fall incidents.

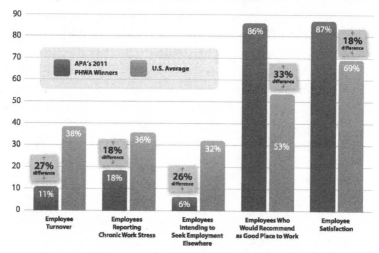

Psychologically Healthy Workplaces Have Lower Turnover, Less Stress and Higher Satisfaction

Sources: American Psychological Association (APA), Psychologically Healthy Workplace Program (PHWP); U.S. Department of Labor, Bureau of Labor Statistics, 2010 Total Separation (with preliminary data for Dec.); APA's 2010 Stress in America and 2011 Work Stress Surveys.
©2011 American Psychological Association

But here's the interesting thing:

Stress isn't the problem!

I'll say it again. Stress is <u>not</u> the problem. Do you know why? Because we can't control the stress. That is the definition of stress: the perception that demands are exceeding our resources. Or a threat, real or imagined. The key word here being "perception." If we could change and control the stress, it wouldn't be stress. So, if stress isn't the problem, what is, you may ask? Good question. It's our reaction to that stress, and <u>that</u>, we can control. We can't control the layoffs, the annoying coworker, the traffic that's making us late for the meeting, or the woman in front of us at the post office that has to look at every stamp ever printed before she finally decides on the flowers. We can't control any of that. But we can control our response to it. And that's what I'm going to teach you to do. Do we want to try to decrease our stress? Sure, absolutely, but as I said, much of it is out of our control.

We also have to remember that different people find different things stressful. For example, for fun I like to ride rollercoasters, go scuba diving, and skydive. I've also swum with sharks and fly regularly on a trapeze. Many people find these things to be incredibly stress inducing. The good stress that we like is called eustress. And as Hans Selye, stress researcher, said, "Stress can only be avoided by dying." Others make the distinction between DIS-stress and stress. We are all predisposed to a certain amount of stress hardiness and we all have different coping mechanisms. Some people thrive on being first responders and have no problem dealing with blood and protruding bones. Others faint at the sign of a needle. To quote Hans Selye again, this time from the *Journal of Extension*, "As I have often said, I don't think anyone should try to eliminate stress; rather you should find your own stress level, find out to what extent you're really sufficiently resistant to keep a certain level of activity. Also, you have to find a goal you can respect—it doesn't matter if other people respect it. You have to have to have enough independence to be your own judge as to whether your aim is right or wrong."

We all have stress just like we all have a temperature. The issue comes when it's out of control. Whatever your level of stress hardiness, we all have to find ways to cope with the stress when it gets out of hand and starts to overtake us. Here, you'll learn easy techniques that you can do on your own at home and at work, for less stress (response). You can take control and not allow stress to be in charge of your life. Thank you for embarking on this journey with me. I'll be here for you every step of the way to make sure you get the most out of this book. It's written for you, to help you be healthier and take full advantage of this phenomenal life we have. Welcome.

And for more tips and tricks to be healthier at work, check out the companion book, *Workplace Wellness*.

Why I Wrote this Book

I started out over two decades ago as a massage therapist. The more my practice grew and the more people I put my hands on, the more I realized that they were coming to me for more than just tight muscles. They started relying on me to be a health practitioner and answer their questions about prescriptions, diseases, and what I thought was wrong with their Uncle Bill. (Not prescribing and diagnosing because I'm not an MD, just to be clear.) I began studying more and more, reading more and more, and I finally decided to formally enhance my training. I got my ND as a traditional naturopath and my Master's and PhD in natural health. The classes that fascinated me most were the mind/body medicine courses and learning about what stress could do. In researching for my dissertation, I had the amazing opportunity to study at the Benson-Henry Institute for Mind/Body Medicine at Harvard. It was an incredible program and really opened my eyes to what power the mind could have over the body.

My dissertation was turned into two books on stress, and as I began to lecture more and do more workshops for industries like nursing, accounting, and 911 dispatchers, I began to really see a need for a comprehensive stress reduction program. And then, an amazing thing happened. I was asked by an old high-school friend to help create a stress-reduction program for the military. And out of that journey, I created the Conquer your Stress program for not only military, but corporations, non-profits, and companies. And this book was born from that. Everything I know about how to destress at work is here. It's my wish that you find things in this book that resonate with you. Maybe not everything will, but take what works. Perhaps it's just one small change you can make. Because as much as I want you to succeed, I also want you to be healthy enough to enjoy it! So enjoy this journey, and please let me know how I can help you going forward.

As a Resource

I am available to hold workshops and assist in the teaching of this material. If your office, corporation, association, or conference can use this type of work, just contact me for more information. I'd love to help.

drkathygruver@gmail.com
www.kathygruver.com
www.corporatestressprograms.com

Warning Signs of Stress

We all assume we know when we are feeling stress, but here's a comprehensive list of "symptoms" that you might not connect to stress:

Physical symptoms:

Headaches, Indigestion
Stomachaches, Sweaty palms
Sleep difficulty, Dizziness
Back pain, Tight neck and shoulders
Racing Heart, Tiredness
Ringing in the ears, Restlessness

Emotional symptoms:

Crying, Nervousness/anxiety
Boredom, Edginess/ready to explode, Anger
Feeling powerless, Unhappy for no reason, Easily upset
Overwhelming sense of pressure, Loneliness

Cognitive symptoms:

Trouble thinking clearly, Forgetfulness
Lack of creativity, Thoughts of running away
Inability to make decisions, Loss of sense of humor
Constant worry

Behavioral symptoms

Excessive smoking, Bossiness
Compulsive gum chewing, Critical attitude of others
Grinding of teeth, Overuse of alcohol
Compulsive eating, Inability to get things done

Work-Specific Warning Signs

In addition to the chart above, some of the warning signs at work are:

Tardiness
Bossiness
Absenteeism
Increased missed work time for illness
Evidence of drug or alcohol use
Increased talk of alcohol or drugs
Missing deadlines
Short temper
Decrease in accuracy of work
Blaming others for mistakes
Sighing
Decreased interest in personal or leisure activities
Violence, physical or verbal
Clumsiness or lack of coordination
Lack of focus, easily distracted

Our bodies seek homeostasis, so for a while we think that the symptoms are normal. That's not true—you have just adapted to accept the headache, the jaw tension, the sleeplessness, and the indigestion. Western medicine often just gives us pills to deal with those symptoms but, in reality, we need to address the root cause and that is often stress.

I did a radio show and the host asked me to go over some of the warning signs of stress, so I listed five or six and there was no response. I had called in to the show and thought maybe we had lost our connection. Finally I hear him mumble, "Uh oh." I asked if everything was okay and he said, "Oh no, I'm stressed. I had no idea. I just thought all of those things were normal."

Get to know your body and your mind so that you know what is normal for you and what isn't. These signs are in place to let you know that something is wrong. And unless you know yourself when you feel good, you won't be able to know how you feel when things start to go awry. Take inventory. We can explain to the mechanic the weird sound that our car is making, but we don't know what is happening inside ourselves. We have to treat ourselves with at least as much respect as we do our car.

The Stress Response

First off, what is stress? One of my favorite definitions is, "A threat, real or imagined." Often, it's something coming from the external world that we think we don't have the resources to deal with. It has a lot to do with feelings of powerlessness, hopelessness, and helplessness. It has been observed throughout time that those three conditions lead to increased disease. From a physiological perspective, it's a cascade of catecholamine hormones, such as adrenaline or noradrenalin, which facilitate immediate physical reactions associated with a preparation for violent muscular action. These include things like an increase in blood pressure and heart and respiratory rate, digestion slowing or stopping, blood rushing to the limbs for action. We may tear up or find our mouths dry, our pupils dilate, sexual response decreases, we may lose hearing or peripheral vision or start to shake. We could lose control of our bowel or bladder. All of these things are useful if we are truly running from a bear, but not when we our perceiving stress at work.

In the stress response, the immune system is at first heightened to help us fight any infection. But if we continue to operate in this heightened state of stress for prolonged periods of time, the immune system starts to weaken and disease can take hold of us. Historically, after the danger passed, hormone levels would decrease and we would sleep. Now, with our stress at a constant level, we don't get that break. This explains the all too common situation of a person who works under constant pressure to meet a deadline and, when she finally allows herself to go on vacation, gets sick on the first day. Her body finally has a chance to rest and the virus can take hold.

A body under stress often has trouble with proper digestion, sleep, sexual function, and nutrient absorption. This is why being in a constantly agitated state is not only bad for our health but leads to more prescriptions and medical interventions. This is bad in the workplace because the stress response also affects our cognitive functioning. Our memory isn't as good, we lose the ability to reason and rationalize, we make more dangerous decisions, and we are more apt to blame others. All of that is going to heighten conflict, lead to more workplace accidents and mistakes, and affect communication.

The opposite of this stress reaction is the Relaxation Response, coined by Dr. Herbert Benson, which calms the stress response and releases feel-good hormones. Whereas the stress response is very helpful in warning us against immediate danger and getting us moving to react, our current stressors are not as dynamic. It's not a saber tooth tiger around the corner that eventually moves away so we can recover; it's the economy, the IRS, our spouse, our job insecurities, our kids, our boss, and other daily stresses that don't seem to subside. These constant, low-grade (or high-grade) stressors don't allow our body the natural downturn in the hormones followed by sleep. When we don't get a break from our reaction to stress, it starts to manifest as problems in our bodies. We also don't often get an outlet for that built-up fight response. As much as we'd like to, we can't punch our boss or physically move the person driving slowly in front of us. So, it builds up more and more and comes out in other aggressive ways or gets buried further in the body and starts to aggravate illness and pain.

Studies have shown that increased use of the Relaxation Response not only slows heart and respiratory rate and decreases blood pressure, but also slows the genetic expression of aging. That's right; relax more, age more slowly. Stress also affects our sleep cycle and brain function. This is why numerous experts from every facet of medicine estimate that 60-80% of our doctor's visits are due to stress-related disease. Some report as high at 90%. The same statistics are applied to workplace accidents.

Another aspect of stress is that our body can't distinguish between what we are imagining and what is happening external to ourselves. This is why we can have dreams that are so real, we wake up scared or mad or guilty that we slept with the neighbor. So, in the same vein, by using our thoughts and fantasizing about something that's not really happening, we can cause a change in our physiology and stress levels. We are actually forming new connections in the brain constantly (called plasticity), and thinking something over and over can change the neural pathways. This is why imagining negative situations or worrying about things that aren't real can make our bodies react so negatively, and why creative visualization and affirmations work.

We have all had experiences where we get ourselves so

worked up over something that we make ourselves sick. This is why it is extremely important to only think positive, productive thoughts. We get enough stress from the outside; we don't need to be making up any more inside our heads. Now that we've talked about stress, let's explore the mind/body connection.

Mind/Body Connection

The mind/body connection is no longer this mysterious, airy-fairy, woowoo concept. Doctors and therapists around the world are recognizing the power of the mind to change our physiology and create our reality. Movies like *The Secret* and *What the Bleep Do We Know* and books like *Think and Grow Rich* tout the power we have in ourselves. Professional athletes visualize their sport and executives are turning to visualizing their business outcomes.

One example of how the mind/body connection works is where our pain and discomfort are in relation to our emotional/spiritual state. In my practice as a massage therapist, I saw first-hand (there's one) a connection between language, our stresses, and our bodies. I've also observed that the area of pain can indicate what is stuck emotionally. I compiled a list of common phrases that we say that are a clear connection between our mental state and what we are manifesting in our body. Here are a few examples (and some common workplace issues):

- Hand and wrist: Get a grip, grasping too tightly, feel like your hands are full.
- Low back: Support issues, feeling spineless, stabbed in the back, sexual issues.
- Lower leg: Moving forward, taking the next step.
- Neck: Who's the pain in the neck?
- Sciatica: Who's the pain in the butt?

If you find that you are having pain somewhere in the body, consider whether it could have a beginning in your mind. Really observe yourself and try to make changes.

Here's a list I've put together of some of the phrases in this society that have body/mind connections. Do any of these sound familiar to you?

A big mouth
A chip on your shoulder
Be on your last leg
Big-hearted
Bone of contention

Broken-hearted
Can't get a handle on it
Can't get a grip
Can't get you out of my head
Can't put my finger on it
Can't stomach it
Cold-blooded
Cold feet
Cold shoulder
Cost an arm and a leg
Cross your mind
Don't have a leg to stand on
Don't have the heart to do it
Elbow grease
Elbow your way in
Elbowroom
From the bottom of your heart
Get a leg up
Getting on my nerves
Get off my back
Get under my skin
Give my right arm for…
Going out of my mind/head
Grab the opportunity
Grasping at straws
Greet someone with open arms
Gut feeling (we've all felt this one, haven't we?)
Have heart
Have no backbone
Have the rug pulled out from under you
Have your back against the wall
He has gall
He's soured to the experience (GERD?)
Heart of gold
Heart set on something
Heart to heart talk
Heartache
Heartbreak
Heartfelt
It's burning me up

It's eating at me (ulcer brewing?)
Jump in with both feet
Keep someone at arm's length
Know it like the back of your hand
Lend a hand
Longs for the sweetness (related to diabetes)
Lose heart
Lump in your throat
Makes me sick to my stomach
Makes my skin crawl
Mouthing off
Moving forward (lower legs)
My hands are full
My heart is blocked (clogged arteries/arteriolosclerosis)
My heart is heavy
My stomach is in knots
No support (back issues)
Now I can breathe easy (feeling of relief, was there asthma
       or bronchitis before?)
Open heart
Open mind
Pain in the ass (piriformis and sciatic issues)
Pain in the neck
Point the finger at someone
Put my foot in my mouth
Put one foot in front of the other
Put your best foot forward
Save face
Shake a leg
Shoot from the hip
Slipped out of my grasp
Someone to lean on
Spineless
Stabbed in the back
Stand on my own two feet
Start off on the wrong foot
Take something to heart
Take your breath away
Tongue-tied
Turn a blind eye

Turn your back on someone
Up to his elbows
Wait on someone hand and foot
Walk the walk
Wears his heart on his sleeve
Weighing on me
Weight of the world is on my shoulders
Welcome someone with open arms
What are you gripping too tightly?
You're such a headache
You've got guts

I also encourage people to avoid saying that something is "killing" them. I don't think that's the best thing to be programming.

We all have times when we have physical pain, and I'm not saying it's 100% of the time connected to the mind. But I have definitely observed it in my clients, family, and even myself. In my experience, if we don't handle the emotions and simply stuff them down, they will find a way to express themselves. And what will get us to pay attention to them is the body. Find someone to confide in, whether a counselor, co-worker, family member, or clergy. It will benefit you for the rest of your life to find a way to acknowledge and process those emotions and stressors.

Stress Solutions:

Breath Work

The basis of any stress reduction program has to start with the breath. Without breath, there is no life. It works on its own, without our conscious control, but it is also in our power to control when we want to. It is often the prime focal point during meditation and mindfulness exercises. Numerous studies link breath control to reduction of PTSD symptoms, emotional regulation, treatment of stress, anxiety and depression, generalized anxiety disorder, response to threat, panic attacks, pain and mood processing, exam stress, feelings of overall wellness, and reducing reactivity to repetitive thoughts.

This section teaches classic deep and rhythmic breathing techniques and emphasizes the pivotal role that breathing plays in relaxation and controlling the stress response.

Let's start with the basic belly breathing. Put one hand on your chest and the other on your belly below the sternum, right above the navel. As you inhale, you should feel the inhalation start in the belly and then to move up into the chest. As you exhale, your belly will move inward towards your back and your chest will drop. Do this in a supine (face-up, lying down) position for the first session, as it's beneficial as you can feel the belly moving more easily. After the first practice, do this sitting in a chair or standing up. Anyone that has ever done public speaking, sung, or played a wind instrument will recognize this as diaphragmatic breathing. It gives us the most power and energy in the breath. And since we have now put it into our control, it becomes a great focal point. Eventually, you will not even have to think about the method of moving the belly during inhalation and exhalation.

Once you can feel the undulating movement of the hands moving up and down as you breathe, make it more rhythmic in nature. Inhale on a count of four, hold for four, then exhale on a count of four and hold for four. As you work with this method, you will be able to easily increase those counts. If holding it for a count of four is comfortable, then try holding for a count of six. Or eight. Breathing in this controlled manner helps contain the stress response, and invokes what Herbert Benson called the Relaxation

Response. And it's harder to have thoughts intrude when we fully put our focus on the breath. When we are in a stressful situation, our breathing quickens and our heart races. This controlled type of breath calms our physiological system and our mind. If you are having trouble mastering this, get a bottle of children's bubbles or breathe through a straw to help control the breath.

This is a great start and something you can do any time, anywhere. When people tell us to breathe and count to 10, yeah, they're right. It calms us down. Once you've mastered this, you can move to the next breath exercise, or stay on this one if you like it.

The second stage of breath work is called square breathing. If you only go as far as the first stage, you will still see enormous benefits, but this takes it a bit further. As you inhale you will form half of the square in your mind, and as you exhale you will form the other half of the square. For example, on the four-count inhale, start in the bottom left corner of the square: 1, 2 will be the horizontal line 3, 4 will be the vertical line. Repeat on the exhale, completing the square. (Or each side of the square is a number: 1, first vertical, 2, horizontal across the top, 3, vertical down, and 4, completing the square). This not only occupies your body but also your mind and calms you further. You may even want to trace the square with your finger as you do this exercise until you can do it without effort; then it becomes a trigger for relaxation, reminding you to relax as you draw the square. Some people draw the square on paper. Or use their finger on their leg, or a table. Some just visualize it, and others draw it on the roof of their mouth with their tongue. Again, adjust the count of the inhale and exhale to whatever timing is comfortable to you without effort. Do whatever works for you! Again, you can stop here or move on to phase three.

The next level of breath work incorporates some light physical movement. This is similar to if you were drawing the square with your finger or hand in the previous exercise. As you inhale, touch your thumb to your other fingers. 1, touch the pointer finger, 2, touch the middle finger, 3, touch the ring finger and 4, touch the pinky finger. And reverse that process for the exhale. This occupies your mind and your body. You can speed up or slow down the breath at whatever pace works for you, and if you feel you have really mastered this, you can do it as you walk, taking a step with every count and every finger movement.

After the basic breath protocol is maintained, it can then be anchored with a daily repeating occurrence, such as teeth brushing, a phone ringing, a bell, before a meal, etc. I use the sound of a bell or chime. No matter where I hear it, it's my cue to pause, just for a brief moment, and breathe. This is a great self-guided technique that can be done at the individual's time of need or directed by a staff person in a group. Even these simple techniques ground us in the present and help our cognitive function, decision-making, communication, and risk taking.

Meditation

Now, for those of you who don't know me, let me explain a bit about me. I'm very type A. My husband describes me as type A+++++. I'm also competitive, anal retentive, a control freak, a Capricorn, an only child, and the daughter of a dad that wanted a son. You can see that I have a lot going against me with this meditation thing. In the past, meditation teachers have told me to quiet my mind and I've laughed out loud. It just doesn't work. I think a lot and I think fast. I also talk and walk fast and I'm a dancer. So shutting off thoughts AND sitting still are big challenges for me. So…when I'm at Harvard and the instructor tells me we're going to meditate, I think, "Oh crap."

I had the misconception that you had to sit on a pillow, legs crossed a certain way, your eyes closed but looking into the center of your own head, you held a finger position, and your tongue was pressing on something, and if you itched you couldn't scratch, and then you floated away in a million bubbles.

But then she tells me the two rules of meditation. (Only two?!)

1. Focus on something repetitive: your breath, a sound, a word, phrase, or mantra.
2. If When a thought comes through, just dismiss it without judgment and continue with what you were concentrating on.

Huh? It's that simple? No shutting off my mind, contorting my body, or holding weird finger positions? Sure, you can do all those things. But the two-rule system works for me. And I found, very quickly, that I could follow those two rules and intruding thoughts ceased, my body relaxed and I didn't want to stop. If I can do it…anyone can do it. Seriously! And remember, this calms our bodies, enhances the immune system, balances our blood pressure, readies our brain for higher functioning, and slows the genetic effects of aging. Why are we not doing this more? This is the perfect follow up to the breath work, as it now engages our thoughts. Traditional meditation (on the pillow) is awesome; we'll get to that in a few minutes, but let's talk about the mini first.

The mini-meditation takes the breath work that has already been learned and simply adds a layer. It adds a repeated word or phrase to the breath. Studies throughout the years certainly support meditation to calm stress and enhance health, but there is also evidence that mantra repetition is beneficial for PTSD, stress management, anger and distress among HIV sufferers, increases mindful attention, increases quality of life and spiritual wellbeing among veterans, and increases hippocampal activity important for memory. This type of meditation not only calms the mind, but also replaces negative thoughts you might be having, as it's not possible to think two thoughts at once. And it has cumulative effects.

This type of mini-meditation can be done in any physical position, at any time; 10-20 minutes per day is recommended. It combines two powerful things, breath and mantra. The key to this is non-judgment. Should other thoughts than the mantra intrude, you just acknowledge, "I'm thinking," and return to the mantra without judgment or frustration, just acknowledgement and a beginner's mind. Once this is practiced and can comfortably be done, this translates into other real life situations. Imagine if you were having a conflict with a co-worker and could stop the judgment (of yourself and them) and just respond rather than react. If you can just observe the feelings and thoughts and take that pause, you become more adaptable to threatening and stressful situations, thus improving relationships, communication, and leadership.

To learn the mini-meditation, get into a comfortable position. This is the easiest way to learn; then, once mastered, it can be done anywhere, at anytime, during any activity, with eyes open or closed. To start, if you are in a safe place to do so, let your eyes gently close. Concentrate on your breath. The movement of the belly in and out, up and down. At any point during this exercise, you can return to your breath as your focal point. On your next inhale think, "I am." And continue to breathe. And with all your inhales, think, "I am." Do that for a few cycles. Then, on your next exhale, think, "at peace." And continue that on all of your exhales. So you are paying attention to your breath and thinking, inhale, "I am," exhale, "at peace." And continue this for five minutes.

If other thoughts intrude, which they often do at first, dismiss them without judgment, return to your breath and thinking, "I am...at peace." This starts to train you to be in the present moment with your concentration fully on your activity and thoughts. This gives us the power to respond rather than react to things in our external environment. Remember: stress is not the problem, it's our reaction to it, and practicing the mini-meditation helps us change that.

There you have it, just a short period of time to erase that detrimental stress response, calm the mind, and enhance the body. I recommend minis to everyone, and this technique can be great for children too; it's so easy to learn.

I use this technique when in traffic (don't close your eyes!), when I find myself stuck at a red light, a few times a day when I feel like I need a little break, before I write or get on stage to prime myself for optimum performance, and sometimes even during a massage when the client is particularly quiet. I use that time to quiet my own mind and do the repetition of (inhale) I am (exhale) at peace.

If the words "I am at peace" do not resonate with you, feel free to substitute other words, whether spiritual, religious, or practical. "I am pure joy," "Jesus loves me," "I am supported," "I am safe," "amen, amen," "Buddha," etc.
And to keep the practice going, reminders can be set to ring at certain intervals, instructing you to stop and do the exercise.

I am in no way an expert on formal seated meditation. I have to say, I can do it now. I attend a silent retreat once or twice a year and can sit for up to two hours on the pillow doing meditation. And all of that is because of the mini. It was my gateway drug to seated meditation. If you want to learn a formal practice, pick which one works for you. There are so many different systems, each varying in intensity and intention. Some are for relaxation and others truly are for communion with the divine and enlightenment. Find a teacher and dive in. But in the meantime, the mini is a great option for immediate and effective change. And if you already have a formal practice, that's awesome. Take what works for you from the mini, if anything, and go for it.

Mindfulness

We talked earlier in the book about doing mini-meditations for health, but there is so much more that can be done in the field of meditation and mindfulness. Just the concept of mindfulness is something that we can incorporate into our work and personal lives. Are you truly present in each moment, or are you mentally pushing the clock and thinking about the date you have that night? I know that it's hard to not let your mind wander to the future or past, but the more present you can be with what you are doing, the better your life will be.

Have you ever gotten to the end of your day and wondered if you've done something that you do every day, like brush your teeth? It's something that we do so unconsciously that it sometimes doesn't even register that we have done it. Have you ever arrived at your destination and suddenly realized you have no recollection of driving there? Such things become so routine that they don't appear in our consciousness. Living life this way is a less than optimal state. It pulls us out of the present moment.

On the other hand, have you ever eaten an entire meal in a present mindful way? Feeling every morsel of food in your mouth, enjoying the textures, scents, and subtle flavors? Try it on a smaller scale. Take a dried cranberry, grape, or cherry and really look at it. Notice the color, the visual texture of it. Then smell it, does it have any odor at all? Then put it in your mouth. Don't bite it yet. Just roll it around in your mouth and see how it feels. Smooth or rough? Is it perfectly round or some other shape? Now slowly bite into it. Does any juice emerge? Is it sweet, bitter, sour? Really taste it. Fully engage with the senses until thought ceases and you are here and only here. That is being mindful.

If we can use mindfulness as an exercise, we can enhance our experiences and train our senses to be more heightened. It also keeps us in the present—and in the present, there is no stress. Stress is in the past in something we are dwelling on or remembering or in the future in something we are worried about or dreading. I had a client the other day remark that her Sunday was terrible. When I asked her why, she said she hates her job so much, all she could think about all day Sunday was how she had to go to work the next day. So, she just ruined a fabulous day of not being at work because of some event in the future. That is no longer the unpleasant boss' fault. It was all on her. What a waste.

Countless studies have been done on mindfulness and its health benefits, including stress reduction and improved recovery, improved PTSD symptoms, reduced anxiety and depression in veterans, better decision making, changes in brain structure, relief of anxiety, more focused attention, and improved sense of well-being. In 2014, Veterans Affairs undertook a review of dozens of studies on the effects of mindfulness, showing positive results for depression, pain, stress, and overall wellness.

The simplest way to teach mindfulness is done with a glass of water or any other beverage. The key is to use all of the senses (sight, touch, taste, smell and hearing) and engage fully. This is about incorporating all the senses to focus the attention in the present. Mindfulness can be done with any activity or object. One task per day for 8-10 minutes is recommended. Non-judgment with this task is important. Mindfulness practice is invaluable at maintaining control over the stress response and enhances decision-making, once again emphasizing responding rather than reacting. This can be done with any task: teeth brushing, showering, washing dishes, or even filing papers. Here is an example of a mindfulness practice. You can record this and listen to it, allowing plenty of time to follow the instructions, or have someone read it to you. Have a beverage handy and begin.

Look at the glass, the bottle, or the cup. What is the shape? How is the light reflecting off of it? How does the liquid look inside, is it clear or does it have a color? Move the glass and observe what that does to the contents. Look at it with one eye closed and then the other. How does it change your view? Is there condensation or water on the outside?

How does the glass feel in your hands? Is it smooth or rough, heavy or light, cold, wet? If you move it slightly, do you feel the reverberation of the liquid inside?

Smell it. Does it have a smell? Breathe it in deeply and try to detect the subtle scents.

Set the glass down and listen for the sound it makes. Hold your ear up to the glass. Does it fizz or make sounds? If you move the glass, can you hear the movement of the liquid against the sides? Are ice cubes clinking?

Hold it up to your lips. How does the container feel against your mouth? Is it cold, hard, rough, smooth? Is there a lip or groove on the glass? Finally, put some in your mouth and let it be there for a few moments. How does it feel in your mouth? Can you hear anything as it exists there? Is it cool on your tongue and roof of your mouth? How does it taste? Take some time to let it be in your mouth before swallowing. And drink it with full awareness.

A variation on this would be to just pick one sense and use it fully. Perhaps you close your eyes and really just pay attention to the sounds around you. Things that you didn't even know were in your environment will suddenly become clear. Can you identify them all? I do this when I get stuck at the crosswalk near my office. Sometimes I'll close my eyes and listen to see if I can tell when the cars stop. Or I'll pick one thing in the environment to really look at. Have you ever really looked at a stoplight? It's pretty amazing.

Here's how mindfulness can help you at work, since this is a book about your workday. Because stress affects cognitive function, memory, reason and logic, risk taking, interpersonal relationships, and communication, stopping the stress enhances all of that. By training yourself to respond rather than react, you are upping your marketable skills for the workplace. If you work with your hands, your work will be more accurate and precise. If you work with your mind, your thoughts will be clearer and more focused. There is no downside to this type of practice.

Another advantage in the workplace is this type of activity makes you more present, more aware, more apt to notice details. You can see the benefits. If you're a nurse, maybe you notice a change in the patient's color. If you're in construction, you may see that one of the bolts is missing in the steel plating. If you are a welder, you might see that a fellow worker is about to knock over a piece of metal that someone accidently left there. When we are more in the moment, we are going to be safer, our coworkers are going to be safer, and we're going to be better at our jobs.

Mindfulness and Communication

I wanted to address something that is a common problem in the workplace. Well, really, anywhere. It's communication and misunderstandings. I conducted a very scientific survey on what people thought the key to communication was (I asked all of my friends on Facebook), and most of them said, "listening." If you look at communication programs and "top ten tips for better communicating," they all start with listening. Of course, that's pretty obvious. But, I have to argue with it a bit. The key to communication is presence. You can't listen if you aren't present or, as I like to say, you can't hear if you're not here.

You must be present with your own emotions, objectives, needs, and wants. You have to know what your preconceptions and your judgments are. You have to know what you are trying to say. This is all the key of Emotional Intelligence. Know Thyself. And you can't do that without presence.

The next step is using concise and accurate words in your initiating the communication. Here's an example:

I say to my husband, "Are you done with this pan?" What is my intention in asking that? I can be more precise to avoid misunderstanding. "Can I put this pan away?" "Is this pan clean?" "If you're done with this pan, can I use it?" "My God, man, clean up after yourself."

If I just say, "Are you done with this pan?" he can choose any of the above interpretations or one I haven't even thought of, and this usually depends on the mood of the receiver. If he's in a bad mood, had a bad day, even if I didn't intend it, he may take it the wrong way. So, being present with our own intentions and choosing our words carefully will clear up many of those misunderstandings and misinterpretations. Also, of course, the tone of the voice is going to influence responses, and some people react to tone and inference more than the actual words.

It's also important for the receiver of the communication to be present and not put a personal spin or misconception on what the initiator just said. This is where responding rather than reacting can come in so handy. I have seen so much conflict arise out of one of the communicators taking things personally, mindreading, misinterpreting, assuming they know what the other means, etc.

We've all been there. Asking questions can clear that up. The boss says he wants to see you on Monday. Rather than wondering what he wants and worrying about it, ask some questions. "Is there anything you need me to prepare for our meeting?" "Is there anything I need to know in advance?" "What do you want to address on Monday so I can get anything together you may need?" He might ignore all your questions and you still might be clueless, but if you don't ask, you will just wonder.

I had the privilege of doing some one on one coaching with an organization in Florida. I spent 15 minutes with select staff and helped them with stress issues, health concerns, and conflict. One woman, I'll call her Beth, came in very upset. The management warned me in advance that Beth had a lot of issues. I ignored that and tried to go in with an open mind and listen without judgment or have their comments coloring my perception. Beth expressed her frustration about not getting a promotion. Management had told her that as soon as the position was open and available, it would be listed for applications but that she would get first shot at it. A few days later, a coworker came up and said, "Hey, did you see that new job is open? I'm going to put in for it." Beth looked online, and, sure enough, the job had been posted for days and the management hadn't told her. She went storming in to her boss's office, told her off, accused her of doing things behind her back, said she didn't want the job anyway, and stormed out. But what Beth didn't realize is the IT department had messed up and posted the job early without letting anyone know. Her boss had no idea it was even listed. The other thing she didn't know is that, though they were encouraging her to submit for that position, they were actually creating a whole other position for her with more responsibility and more money. But after her outburst, they trashed the idea and left her where she was.

By her reacting rather than taking a bit to respond, she blew her chances at the job she claimed to want. Had she walked into her boss' office and said something to the effect of, "Hey, I saw that job was listed, I'm really disappointed you didn't let me know," the boss would've had the ability to explain the situation and the employee would've gotten what she wanted. Don't be Beth.

I can go on for pages about communication and presence and responding rather than reacting, but there's not time. We have to learn some more techniques. The last thing I'll say is about communication styles. There are so many systems of personality types and different styles of interacting, everything from colors to initials. The one that seems the most important is direct and indirect. I'm very direct. "Do you want the 3pm massage?" If I get a simple "no" back, I'm very happy. Often what I get is, "I'd really like to, but I have to take my dog to the groomers. I've had him for years, and, sure enough, every summer he runs into brambles. No, they're not really brambles, they're more like burrs. These really sticky things, so every year I have to take him to the groomer and 3 is the only time I can. What else do you have?"

As a direct communicator, this drives me crazy. I don't need a monologue, I don't want to hear the back-story, I want to know if you want the appointment. But, because I can't yell at every person that does that to me, I have learned who in my sphere is direct, who is indirect, and I base my interaction on that. So, rather than writing back, "How about 4?" I say, "Bummer, so sorry to hear that. What a pain. We do love our pets though. How about 4, would that give you enough time?" This satisfies their need for an exchange and I also get my direct question in. This takes practice…and patience. But I know you can do it!

I'm also pretty darn bubbly and outgoing, so if I run up to a more reserved introvert with my full energy, I'm going to scare the crap out of them and they're going to have less ability to hear me. I've learned to pull from aspects of my personality and shape-shift to what is going to benefit the person most. Awareness and adaptability is key here.

Affirmations, the Power of Words

In learning to change our minds and be present, I've found one of the simplest and most effective techniques is using affirmations. Some experts estimate that we have around 60,000 thoughts a day and 50,000 of those are negative. That's 80% negative thoughts, which translates to me as 80% negative results. It's so easy, especially with what's happening in the world today, to let our thoughts go to fear, worry, and fatalism. And it is important to acknowledge our feelings and note that we do have fear and concern, but when these thoughts start to rule our minds and become repetitive and distorted, as we talked about in the previous chapters, it can lead to illness, negative changes in our bodies, and poor work outcomes.

If we look at our life at this exact second, where is the stress? Seriously, look at this moment in time. What is wrong? Our thoughts, and thus our stress, are often in the future, and usually about something that we're not even sure is going to happen. We talk about it, think about it, and dwell on it even if it's not guaranteed. Like we learned before, we can't control our emotions, but we can control our thoughts. I'll teach you another way to do that. We've talked about emotion/body correspondence, mindfulness, mini-meditations, and the stress response. The next technique is affirmations, using positive language to program our lives.

I find this especially useful when negative thoughts interfere with our ability to fall asleep. Try repeating the following phrase, "I fall asleep quickly and easily, I wake up feeling refreshed." These types of short phrases do one of two things. Either they program me to fall asleep quickly and wake up feeling refreshed or, at the very least, they shut out the other thoughts that are running through my head. There is a physics axiom that states, "Two solid objects cannot occupy the same space at the same time." The same principle applies with our thoughts. We can't be thinking two things at once. That's what counting sheep is all about; it distracts us from those repetitive thoughts that plague us at bedtime. I'm not saying changing our thoughts and words is easy. On the contrary, it can be quite hard at first, especially if we have been programmed to think negatively since we were young or are surrounded by negativity in our lives. But it can be done with a little practice, and the results are phenomenal.

When working with affirmations there are a few rules of thumb:

Make them short.
Keep them in the present tense.
Make them positive.
And repeat often!

So, don't say, "I'm not sick anymore." Rephrase your wording to, "I am healthy and well." Saying, "I want to be rich," puts the emphasis on the future and focuses on a current state of lack. Saying, "I am wealthy and abundant," or, "Money flows easily to me from unexpected sources," creates a positive, present-time scenario.

Affirmations can be repeated silently throughout the day, put up on a mirror, carried in a purse or pocket as a reminder, or posted in a common area for all to see. Using affirmations doesn't only make changes in our physiology and external environment, but at the very least stops the stress response, which has enormous benefit. And affirmations have the fake it 'til you make it quality. Even if you don't believe it at first, you are rewiring your brain to have more positive thoughts. It doesn't cost anything to do, there are no side effects, you don't need a prescription, and it feels good!

To create affirmations for you, the first task is to recognize where you tend towards negative thinking and negative self-talk. For example, if it has to do with running, if you find you are being hard on yourself or beating yourself up that you can't run as far or fast as everyone else, examine that self-talk to see what you're saying. Perhaps the words, "I'll never be as fast as him," keep entering your consciousness. Or you're simply thinking, "I'm so slow." Change those words to make them positive and in the present: "I am fast and nimble," "I win the race," "I am a gazelle" (and with that last one you can actually add visualization to picture yourself as a gazelle). When at a sales call, breathe and say, "I sign this contract," "I make this sale," "I am accurate and precise in my communication." These can be customized to use whatever phrases would work. Here are a few samples for different scenarios:

- Health: I am healthy and well, my immune system is strong and resilient, I fight off the infection, I am free of illness, I am strong and fit.
- Sports performance: I win, I conquer, I succeed, I am a winner, I overcome, I am strong and fast.
- Sleep: I fall asleep quickly and easily, I wake up feeling refreshed, sleep comes easily to me.
- Social: I am surrounded by supportive people, I am loved, I am appreciated, I am enjoyable to be around, I have many friends.
- Productivity: I meet all my goals and deadlines with ease, I have plenty of time, my work is easy, I finish in plenty of time, I am accurate in my work.
- Mood: I am happy and carefree, I am filled with joy, I am filled with love, light follows me, I am filled with the grace of God.
- Fear: I am strong, I am brave, I overcome, I am divinely supported, I do it, I am protected.
- Physical pain or discomfort: I am comfortable, I am calm, I am in control of my body, my body's natural state is wellness, I feel fabulous.

There are endless categories and endless affirmations.

It's easy to incorporate affirmations into your life. Take some time to work these into your day by saying them at a certain set time (maybe when you wake up or before you go to sleep) or keeping them posted on your mirror, car dashboard, or desktop. Once affirmations become part of your life, you'll be more in tune with when your thinking and words have become negative and you'll automatically change them to positive statements. Going in to situations with a negative attitude doesn't benefit anyone and just makes life more unpleasant. And it ups our stress response and negatively affects life at work and home.

And if you believe in the power of positive thought, you won't just be changing your mind; you'll be changing your external circumstances. Many people believe that we can create opportunities and success for ourselves with the power of our minds. I have seen it happen in my own life, and in the lives of those around me. If nothing else, besides reducing the stress response, it actually makes us more positive. And more positivity allows us to be more open to experiences and opportunities. Try it; what have you got to lose?

Creative Visualization,
Using Your Imagination for Success

Studies show that visualization can help with stress, pain, anxiety, sleep, grief, decision making, enhancing performance endurance, and the like. Visualization is so powerful that it can actually have an effect on physical responses such as blood flow to the limbs, blood pressure, and asthma. We can heal quicker using our minds.

Visualization and using the imagination for stress reduction is one of the most powerful tools. The mind cannot tell the difference between what is being thought about and what is really happening. So, if you can extract yourself from an emotionally stressful situation and be mentally located in a safe place, the reactions will change and therefore increase flexibility during stressful situations. Mastering this skill will allow you to calm yourself mentally very quickly, thus enabling better decision making and quicker reactions. Simple visualizations of nature or finding one's safe place can be guided live in a group, taught one on one, or done with prerecorded apps. Eventually with practice, no guidance will be necessary and you can take yourself on a personalized journey whenever needed

There are two choices as to how visualization can be used. The first is simply being guided through a safe and beautiful place, like taking a vacation in your mind. The other one is actually visualizing for performance or healing. For example, if you are about to shoot darts, you would visualize yourself getting a bull's-eye. Or, if you have a broken leg, you can visualize the bone healing quicker. You can visualize a meeting going well and the boss smiling at you. Don't we visualize on a daily basis anyway, every time we daydream or fantasize?

I first learned about visualization when I was working on a community theatre production of *Oklahoma*. During a break in rehearsal, an older Chinese man was showing tricks with playing cards. I mentioned to him that I thought I was getting sick because my throat was starting to hurt. He asked if I ever did visualization. (I was sixteen, what did I know?) I told him I didn't think so.

He explained to me that when he is starting to feel like he is coming down with something, he activates his immune system by visualizing it. He pictures the white blood cells swarming to an area like the cavalry coming over the hill to save the day. He would lie quietly in bed and just imagine these creatures rushing to help. And often, he would feel better and not get sick. And he said that kind of visualization could help with anything. I tried it that night, visualizing my white blood cells rushing to my throat to help and white light filling my neck. I woke up the next day pain-free and didn't get sick. And I was brilliant as Chorus Girl Number Three in *Oklahoma.*

I used this technique for much more important things as my life went on. Since I'm big on personal examples, here's a good one.

I was a freshman in college, auditioning to be a dancer on a cruise ship. I was warming up and kicking very high over my head when my other foot came out from underneath me and I fell right on my tailbone. I got off the floor and just kept warming up and then proceeded to dance for a few hours. Later, I felt severe pain. I couldn't stand or sit for any period of time. That Monday, I went to the doctor, who informed me after an x-ray that I had cracked a vertebra and they weren't sure how serious it was yet, but they wanted to do some more tests. I was then scheduled for a 360° bone scan and told I might need to wear a back brace for six months. That did not make me happy.

This was where visualization came in. Every night, I would picture that x-ray of my spine and picture the vertebrae, and a little man dressed like a construction worker would show up and use his caulking gun to fill in the crack. He looked like the guy from Super Mario Bros™. I saw my white blood cells rushing there too and then also pictured warm, healing light. I did this every night with my hands on my low back.

I noticed the pain had subsided, but still needed Tylenol and ice occasionally. It also seemed that I had more range of motion and could sit longer. I returned to the doctor for my bone scan. Two days after the procedure, I sat in his office dreading the news that I would need to be confined to a brace. He put the x-ray up on the light screen and next to it, the bone scan. He counted down the vertebrae in the x-ray and said, "See, here is the crack." He then pointed to the bone scan "and you can see the crack here…" and then he stopped. He double-checked the name on the x-ray and counted the vertebrae in both images. They both were mine and the images were identical. With one exception: the crack was gone. My dad looked at me. The doctor looked at me and said, "I don't know what you did, kid, but you just saved yourself six months of discomfort," and I went home. It took a bit longer for the pain to be totally gone, and I will admit that it is still a weak area in my body. Too much dancing or a bad mattress and I'll feel it, but this remarkable experience made me realize what the power of the mind could do to the body.

I have worked with cancer sufferers who use this type of visualization. Whether they picture angels coming to take away the tumor or bugs slowly eating it away, it has been proven to help our bodies heal. It is important to come up with an image that works for you. I read a story about a woman in a cancer support group where they were visualizing the body attacking the cancer and doing battle with it. One woman in the class was having no results and was actually starting to have anxiety over the experience. It turned out she witnessed much war when she was a child and found those images offensive and not healing. When she was allowed to pick her own non-violent visuals, she started to see great results. This is why it's important to customize this to what works for YOU. So, the type of visualization mentioned above is for health and healing. The second one, in the next chapter, goes beyond health and can change your life.

Visualization for Achievement

So, I mentioned visualization and imagery for healing and stress reduction, but other than that, how does that help at work? Well, I'm so glad you asked. There are some that believe, in the same vein as affirmations, that we can change our external circumstance and outcomes by what we think. So, visualize the new car, the perfect job, or the amazing mate. And perhaps you will get those things. I have heard success story after success story about that exact thing. And in the world of sports, you think that kicker isn't visualizing the football splitting the uprights? You bet he is! (Go Steelers!)

But even if you don't believe that's possible, how about this: you have an important meeting and you are thinking about it and you start to worry that it might not go so well, and you think about how maybe you're not really right for the job, and what if the boss doesn't really like you, and you start a whole movie in your head about how awful it's going to be, and you start to feel sick and you start to get stressed and then you have to walk in to that meeting. How is that going to work out for you? Probably not so well.

On the contrary, you think about this meeting and you visualize the boss smiling and congratulating you, shaking your hand and welcoming you to your fabulous new position. You start to feel confident and happy. You feel strong and accomplished. Now you walk in to the meeting. Better, huh?

Because now, even if you don't get what you want, you will be better equipped to handle it. And you haven't built yourself up to a state of negativity. Why suffer twice? If things go awry, you can suffer then. Why suffer in your mind before the event even takes place? This is where visualization is fabulous. Keep your thoughts and daydreams positive. There is no downside. And who knows, you might even achieve your dreams. I have to admit, pretty much everything I achieved, I visualized first.

Progressive Muscle Relaxation

This is sort of a bonus technique for you and it's incredibly simple but useful for calming the mind and the body. This involves starting with a part of the body, typically the feet, and concentrating on relaxing that part of the body, just imaging soothing comfort and calm in that area, then moving up to the calves and then the thighs, etc. You move progressively up the body, taking body part by body part, focusing on them and relaxing them. This helps you pay attention to the stress in those parts of the body and helps to dissipate it. This technique that was created in the 1920s has been useful for such things as irritable bowel syndrome, headaches, and general tension. This is also a great way to relax to fall asleep or get rid of tension in your body during the day.

Here is a sample script/protocol for progressive muscle relaxation. Feel free to record this for yourself, have someone read it to you, or, once you're familiar enough with it, you can just run through it in your head.

Get into a comfortable position; sitting or lying down is best. Start by concentrating on the breath and doing just a few mini-meditations; inhale (I am), exhale (at peace). No matter how relaxed you become, you will stay in the chair or comfortably in the position you are in. Now send your focus to your feet. Which foot feels different? Just think about that. Think of the feet relaxing, feeling the floor under your feet or your feet in space as you lie flat. Now, that feeling of relaxing and calm moves up past the feet and encircles the ankles. It moves up the calves and the shins and they relax more deeply. With every exhale, the lower limbs relax just a bit more. With your next inhale, you send that relaxation up through your thighs and you feel those become soft, calm, and relaxed. With every inhale, you breathe in positivity and with every exhale the stress and tension of the day, week, month, and year just fade away. The feeling of relaxation that started in the feet and moved up from the feet, ankles, lower legs, and thighs now moves up into the hips and those relax. The low back relaxes; more room occupies the space between the vertebrae. Any discomfort you feel in your body as you move up the spine just fades away. The tension melts away. The feeling moves up to the lower abdomen and your stomach muscles relax. You feel your breathing deepen a bit more. With your next cycle of breath, that feeling of calm and control moves into the chest and the breath deepens as your lungs feel clear and powerful. Your entire body relaxes more with each breath. The feeling of relaxation in your lower limbs, hips, and chest moves up into your shoulders, you feel the tension melt away, and you may feel the shoulders drop a bit as all the stress and anxiety leaves that area of your body. That relaxation that started in the feet, moved up the legs to the hips, the back, to the chest, and into the shoulders now moves out across the arms and you feel your hands relax, each individual finger relaxes with every exhale. That feeling of calm and control that is in your shoulders now moves up your neck and your neck relaxes even more with every exhale. It doesn't even feel the weight of your head; it just exists in its own space. And with the next inhale, you breathe in more relaxation and calm and the next exhale sends that relaxation up over the head, and the scalp relaxes, the facial muscles relax, the tongue relaxes in the mouth, your lips may part slightly, and the corners of your eyes feel even heavier. So now, from the bottom of your feet to the top of your head, you are relaxed, filled with calm, and in control. With every exhale, you relax further and release the tensions of the moment, day, week, month, and year. It all fades away and you find yourself fully present in the now with your breath and your fully relaxed body. Your body is comfortable, relaxed, calm, peaceful, present, and feeling good all over. Remember, you can access this at any time by thinking of the word 'calm.' And in a few moments, I will bring you back to the present moment, where you will find yourself refreshed and energized, peaceful, and fully in the present, taking with you the good and positive feelings from this experience. And on 0 you tend to relax just a bit more. 1, you are aware of your body in the chair or on the surface it's on. 2, you are aware of your body in the room. 3, you start to become more conscious of the environment around you. 4 is a very alert number, and 5 is eyes open, wide awake. 1, 2, 3, 4, 5, awake and alert, feeling positive and calm.

Create an Environment for Less Stress

I had a client who was incredibly stressed out. She was a financial advisor and managed people's millions. She was working 10 or 12-hour days, not leaving her desk, not eating lunch, and generally going crazy. She was not productive, not sleeping, and stressed beyond belief. She came to me for a stress management session. I asked her when her last vacation was, and it had been three or four years ago. I asked her where her favorite vacation spot was, and she said it was Hawaii; sitting on the beach was her perfect escape.

She had the advantage of having her own office space with a door. I asked her if she was allowed to do whatever she wanted to do with that space, and she answered in the affirmative. I told her to go ahead and paint the walls, make them a nice sea blue or something that reminded her of the sky. I advised her to put a photo on her desk of herself at the beach, or better yet, her legs looking out towards the ocean as if she were sitting in a chaise lounge. I also had her buy a scented candle that smelled like the ocean or coconut, whatever got her in that relaxing place. She also bought a sound machine that had the sound of the ocean. I asked her if she had a computer; she answered that she had two. I asked her what her backdrop was on the computer; she said that swirly thing that came with the computer. I told her to get rid of the swirly thing and get scenes of the ocean or the beach or palm trees. And the final piece, and this was many years ago, I asked her if she had one of those big old desks with the drawer to the right for files that is now filled with crap. She said she did. I asked her what was in that drawer. She answered, "Crap." I told her to take the crap out and put in a bucket filled with sand. So, whenever she needed to, she could turn on the sound machine, light the candle, stare at the picture frame or the computer and put her hand in the bucket of sand. We managed to bring Hawaii to her. And again, because the brain thinks what we are fantasizing about is real, it took her on a vacation in her office.

Even if you don't have your own office space or if you're in a job that doesn't have an office, you have the ability to have something as a reminder that takes you to your relaxing space. Perhaps it's something in your car so that as you drive to and from work, you can take an extra minute to relax either before or after your work time. Maybe you have something in your purse or an app on your phone that is a reminder, a trigger that it's time to relax. Something on your key ring or in your truck. The list of possibilities is endless, if you think about it. We are living in a time where stress is higher than ever, and if we can take those moments of what we need to remind us to go to our special place, we are going to have an advantage.

Conclusion

It truly is my hope that the suggestions I made will help you to be healthier, more productive, and successful. Remember that you have the power. You have a choice as to where you put your focus, what thoughts you allow to enter your mind, and how you respond to the things around you. You truly can change your mind to change your life.

Let me know how I can help you going forward. My passion is to educate people, to empower and inspire them. If I can help in anyway, don't hesitate to contact me.

And have a healthy day!

About the Author

Kathy Gruver, PhD is a motivational speaker, an award-winning author, and hosts the national TV show based on her first book, *The Alternative Medicine Cabinet* (Winner Beverly Hills Book Awards). She has earned her PhD in Natural Health and has authored five books, including *Body/Mind Therapies for the Bodyworker*, *Conquer Your Stress with Mind/Body Techniques* (Winner Indie Excellence Awards, Beverly Hills Book Awards, Global E-book Awards, Irwin Awards, Finalist for the USA Best Books Award), *Journey of Healing* (Winner USA Best Book Awards, Beverly Hills Book Awards, Pinnacle Awards, Indie Excellence Awards, and the non-fiction category of the London Book Festival) and she co-wrote *Market My Practice*.

She has studied mind/body medicine at the famed Benson-Henry Institute for Mind-Body Medicine at Harvard Medical School and has been featured as an expert in numerous publications, including *Glamour*, *Fitness*, *Time*, *More*, *Women*, *Wall Street Journal*, CNN, WebMD, Prevention, *Huffington Post*, Yahoo.com, *Marie Claire*, *Ladies Home Journal*, Dr. Oz's *The Good Life*, and *First*. Dr. Gruver has appeared as a guest expert on over 250 radio and TV shows, including NPR, SkyNews London, Every Way Woman, Morning Blend in Las Vegas, CBS Radio, and Lifetime Television, and has done over 150 educational lectures around the world for everyone from nurses in the Middle East to 911 dispatchers in New Orleans, corporations around the US, and teachers in her own backyard. She was thrilled to appear on the TEDx stage in February. She just completed work on a project for the military to create and institute a stress-reduction program. For fun and stress relief, Dr. Gruver does flying trapeze and hip hop dance.

A past winner of NAWBO's Spirit of Entrepreneurship Awards, Dr. Gruver maintains a massage and hypnotherapy practice in Santa Barbara, California. She has also produced an instructional massage DVD, *Therapeutic Massage at Home: Learn to Rub People the RIGHT Way*™, and is a practitioner with over 25 years of experience. More information can be found at www.thealternativemedicinecabinet.com.

Made in the USA
Columbia, SC
13 October 2021

46851789R10029